From the Nation's #1 Educational Publisher K-12

Grade 2

Enrichment Reading

Challenging and Fun Activities
Critical Thinking • Problem Solving
Creative Thinking • Comprehension

Table of Contents

Table of Contents (continued)

Credits:

McGraw-Hill Consumer Products Editorial/Production Team
Vincent F. Douglas, B.S. and M. Ed.
Tracy R. Paulus
Jennifer Blashkiw Pawley

Warner Bros. Worldwide Publishing Editorial/Production Team
Michael Harkavy   Charles Carney
Paula Allen   Allen Helbig
Victoria Selover   Holly Schroeder

Design Studio
Cover: Beachcomber Studio
Interior: Color Associates

Illustrators
Cover & Interior: Animated Arts!™

McGraw-Hill
Consumer Products
A Division of The McGraw-Hill Companies

Send all inquiries to:
McGraw-Hill Consumer Products
250 Old Wilson Bridge Road
Worthington, Ohio 43085

1-57768-292-0   1 2 3 4 5 6 7 8 9 10 QPD 04 03 02 01 00 99

MATHEMATICS ACTIVITY

Find the Objects

Find and count the benches, kites, pigeons, and dogs in the picture. Write the numbers on the lines.

‎2‎ benches

‎‎ dogs

‎‎ pigeons

‎‎ kites

3

LANGUAGE ACTIVITY

Sentence Mix-Ups

Unscramble the words in each group to make a sentence. The first word in each sentence is in the right place. Write each sentence on the lines.

1. My checkup today is.

   My checkup is today.

2. The my takes pulse nurse.

3. I getting like shots don't.

4. A reward a good is candy bar.

LANGUAGE ACTIVITY

Make a Word

Draw a line from the sidecar to each motorcycle to complete a word.

art

and

at

are

ar

 k	 w	 m	 n
d	j	 l	 g

5

By the Sea

Find out how many of each animal are in the sea.

Fill in one square for each animal you count.

5					
4					
3					
2					
1	▨				

PROBLEM SOLVING ACTIVITY

Go Home

Use your finger to trace a path through the maze to connect The Brain to the lab. Then use a green crayon to mark the path. Use a different colored crayon for the paths of each of the other characters.

Can you help The Brain go to the (lab)?

Can you help Slappy get to her 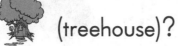 (treehouse)?

Can you help Dot get to the 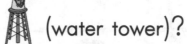 (water tower)?

CRITICAL THINKING ACTIVITY

What Is In It?

Identify each object on the left and determine which object in the row would most logically be inside. Circle your choices.

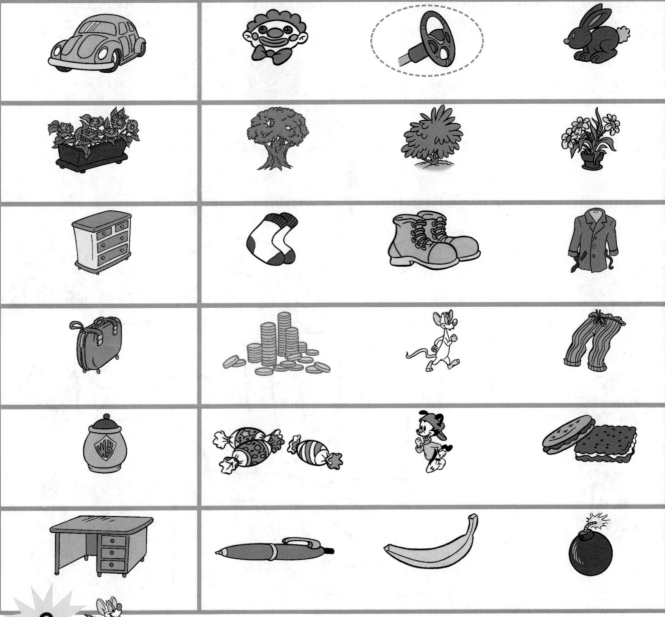

LANGUAGE ACTIVITY

Moon Code

Each symbol used below stands for a letter. Use the code. Write the words. Then say the words.

1.

u	b	r	g
●	◗	◖	○

b u g

2.

n	e	a	m	g
○	◡	◐	●	◗

3.

k	h	s	f	i
☽	◗	☾	◖	○

ORAL PRESENTATION

What Did You See?

Write a paragraph about your favorite movie. Read your paragraph to a friend or family member.

PROBLEM SOLVING ACTIVITY

On the Farm

Read each sentence. Then draw a picture showing the sentence.

1. Corn is growing behind the fence.

2. A bird has laid 10 eggs in her nest.

3. A pig is eating from a trough.

4. A pail of milk is on the ground.

5. A dog sits beside the barn door.

Toys for Sale

Write **Yes** or **No.** Then tell how much change you will get or how much more you need.

 45¢

 80¢

 75¢

 60¢

95¢

50¢

25¢

15¢

1. You have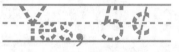

   Can you get a clown doll?

   Yes, 5¢

2. You have

   Can you get two paddles with balls?

3. You have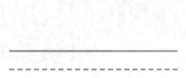

   Can you get a slingshot?

(continued)

Toys for Sale

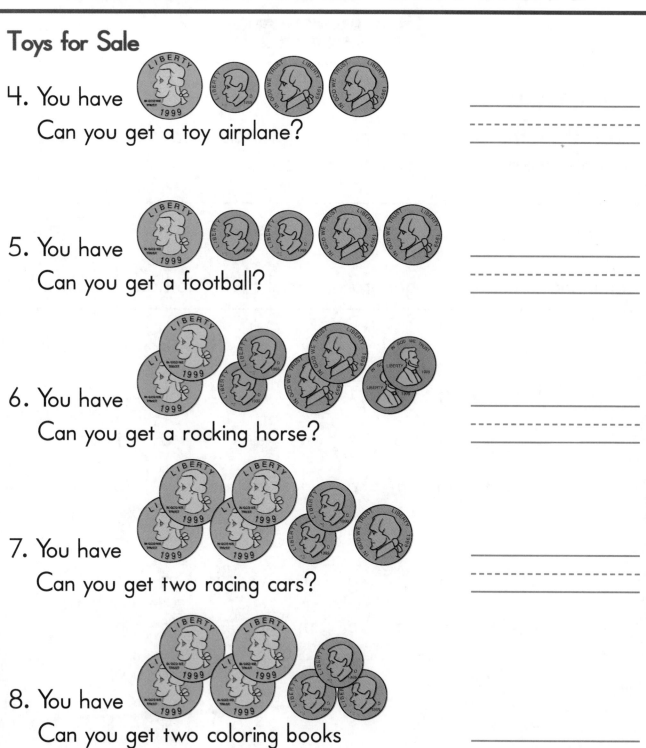

4. You have
   Can you get a toy airplane?

   _____
   - - - - - - - - - - -
   _____

5. You have
   Can you get a football?

   _____
   - - - - - - - - - - -
   _____

6. You have
   Can you get a rocking horse?

   _____
   - - - - - - - - - - -
   _____

7. You have
   Can you get two racing cars?

   _____
   - - - - - - - - - - -
   _____

8. You have
   Can you get two coloring books
   and crayons?

   _____
   - - - - - - - - - - -
   _____

PROBLEM SOLVING
ACTIVITY

Find a Word

Find each of the words in the puzzle and circle them. Words are written vertically, horizontally, and diagonally.

giant	world	speech	cage	captain	system
command	control	general	night	method	boss

```
c  e  j  m  s  y  s  t  e  m
n  i  g  h  t  p  m  r  t  s
w  y  o  g  e  n  e  r  a  l
c  o  m  m  a  n  d  e  y  u
o  a  r  s  e  t  f  e  c  z
n  l  p  l  g  t  w  m  g  h
t  h  e  t  d  m  h  y  h  b
r  s  g  i  a  n  t  o  t  o
o  p  y  h  s  i  s  i  d  s
l  l  c  a  g  e  q  n  r  l  s
```

LANGUAGE ACTIVITY

What Is My Name?

Each letter of the alphabet has a symbol. Use the code to make names. Write the names.

A	B	C	D	E	F	G	H	I
○	□	△	☆	ᴍ	⊞	⊙	◇	☺

J	K	L	M	N	O	P	Q	R
◩	⌇	▽	▢	✛	✕	⋈	◑	♡

S	T	U	V	W	X	Y	Z	
⊕	⊚	▣	▽	⊠	⊓	⇧	⇩	

Write your name in code. _____

LANGUAGE ACTIVITY

Crack the Code

There are many different kinds of codes. Crack each coded message below. Read the clues to help you.

1. REWOT RETAW EHT TA EM TEEM

   Clue: This message is written backwards.

   Meet me at the water tower.

2. WEA RAC LEV ERD ISG UIS E

   Clue: The spaces between the words are in the wrong place.

3. EP OPU XBLF VQ UIF HVBSE

   Clue: Change each letter to the one that comes before it in the alphabet.

4. 8-5 23-9-12-12 2-5 13-1-4

   Clue: The number *1* stands for *A*, *2* stands for *B*, and so on. Write the alphabet under the numbers 1-26.

Use these codes to write your own secret messages to a friend. Then make up your own codes to share.

RESEARCH AND REPORTING ACTIVITY

Tell All About It

You know that a library has many kinds of books. It has story books, books that give information, and books about real people.

Go to the library and read a book of your choice. You can ask the librarian to help you pick out a book. Tell the librarian what kind of book you would like to read.

Fill out the form below to tell about your book.

Title _____

Author _____

Kind of Book _____

What the Book is About _____

_____

_____

_____

My Favorite Part _____

_____

_____

_____

CRITICAL THINKING ACTIVITY

The Name Game

Work with a friend to make a name book.

First write down all the letters, A to Z. Then think of all the names you know that begin with A. Go on to B, C, and all the others.

Count up all the names for each letter. Color in one box for each name.

A
B
C
D
E
F
G
H
I
J
K
L
M

N
O
P
Q
R
S
T
U
V
W
X
Y
Z

What letters have the most names? Is there a letter with no names? How many names begin with the same letter as yours?

Ask your family to tell you why they gave you your name. Tell the story to your friends.

CREATIVE THINKING ACTIVITY

Pinky

Who Am I?

Here is a guessing game you can play in a group. The name of the game is "What's My Name?"

One player thinks of a person everyone knows. It can be a real person, or it can be a character from a book, movie, or television show.

Then the player gives a few clues to help the others guess the name. Can you guess the name from the clues below?

My face is in a monument.
I had a beard and wore a tall hat.
I was a president.
I was very honest.

The other players take turns guessing. If no one can guess, the players can ask for another clue. The first player to say the right name gets to be the next mystery person.

CRITICAL THINKING ACTIVITY

Which Is It?

Look at these cakes. They all look the same, don't they? One cake is different. Look again, closely. Find the cake that is different. Then circle the two things that make it different.

LANGUAGE ACTIVITY

Picture This

Did you know that you can write messages using pictures? A *rebus* is a kind of puzzle that uses pictures for words. Can you figure out what each rebus below says? Write the word under each picture.

ch +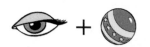

 +

 + + th

cheer

Now write what this rebus says.

    in a   .

 tr + + d 2 b +   .

   + her   t + .

 will   .

Try to make your own rebus. Leave spaces between the words. Use a + sign to link sounds that make one word. Give your rebus to a friend to figure out.

Swimming Fish

Mobiles are kinds of art work that can move in the wind. You can make your own mobile of fish swimming.

You Will Need

colored construction paper

thread

scissors

a wire hanger

1. First make six fish using different colored construction paper. Fold a piece of paper in half. Cut along the dotted lines as shown in the picture. Open up your paper and you have a fish! Draw a mouth and an eye on each side of your fish.

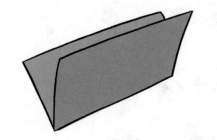

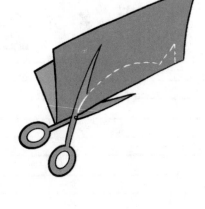

(continued)

ART ACTIVITY

Swimming Fish

2. Cut a long piece of thread. Use a pencil to make a hole in each fish. Move the point around until the hole is big enough for the thread. Put one end through the hole and tie a knot. Be careful not to tie your finger—you're way too heavy for the mobile.

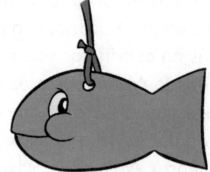

3. Now it is time to put your mobile together. Tie each fish to the wire hanger. Before you make knots, hold up the hanger and see if your mobile is balanced. You can pull on the thread to make the fish hang longer or shorter. You can also move the thread from side to side.

Move your fish until your mobile is balanced. Then tie a knot to keep each fish in place.

4. Hang up your mobile in a place where there is a little breeze so you can watch your fish swim!

SCIENCE ACTIVITY

Just Tasting

Sometimes you use different senses at the same time. Do you think you use only your sense of taste when you eat? Here is a way you can find out.

You will need some bite-sized pieces of food that are all crunchy, like an apple, carrot, turnip, and raw potato. You can try creamy things, too—ice cream, pudding, yogurt, and mashed potatoes.

This is an activity for you to do with one or more friends. One of you needs to cover your eyes with a cloth and hold your nose. Someone puts a piece of one of the foods in your mouth. You try to guess what it is. Take turns so each of you gets a chance to test your tasting sense. Write down which foods were the hardest to guess.

Try this with things you drink, too. See if anyone can guess which is orange juice and which is grapefruit juice. Make sure you cover your eyes and hold your nose.

What does this tell you about tasting? Do you use only your sense of taste when you eat, or are other senses important, too? Is your sense of taste linked more to your sight or smell?

MATHEMATICS ACTIVITY

Making Change

You can practice making change with a friend or family member by playing the game below.

You Will Need: cardboard, scissors

First, make coins by cutting out circles for pennies, nickels, dimes, and quarters. Write 1¢, 5¢, 10¢, or 25¢ on each coin. Each of you should have ten pennies, five nickels, three dimes, and two quarters.

To play, one of you starts by making up a problem, such as this one:

> I bought something that cost 33 cents.
> I gave the salesman one quarter and one dime.
> How much change did I get?

As you say the problem, show your partner the coins you used. Your partner has to add up the coins and make the right change. Did you figure out that the answer to this problem is two cents change?

Take turns giving problems and making change. Each time you make the right change, you get one point. The player with the most points wins the game.

SOCIAL STUDIES ACTIVITY

Wave the Flag

The flag of the United States has 13 stripes and 50 stars. The 13 stripes stand for the first 13 states. The 50 stars stand for the 50 states we have today. Did you know that every country in the world has its own flag?

Use an information book in the library to help you find a picture of a flag from another country. Draw the flag in the box. Write the name of the country on the line.

Did you know that every state also has its own flag? Find a picture of your state flag and draw it in the box. Write the name of your state on the line.

Even your school can have a flag! Make up a flag for your school and draw it in the box. Write the name of your school on the line.

CRITICAL THINKING ACTIVITY

What Do You Think?

Pretend that your family is thinking about buying a computer. Think of reasons why you would like to have a computer. What would you use a computer for? Taking over the world? Keeping track of Pinky's thoughts? How would other people in your family use the computer? If you already have a computer, think about why you like having one.

Also think of reasons why you might not like to have a computer. Would the computer be hard to share? Would the computer take too much time away from doing other things? If you already have a computer, are there any things you do not like about it?

Write down your reasons on the lines below. Use another sheet of paper if you need to.

Why I Would Like to Have a Computer (or)
Why I Like Having a Computer

_____

- -

_____

- -

_____

Why I Would Not Like to Have a Computer (or)
Why I Do Not Like Having a Computer

_____

- -

_____

- -

_____

CREATIVE THINKING ACTIVITY

Box by Box

Drawing on a computer is not the same as drawing on paper. The pictures that you see on a computer are made up of hundreds of little boxes. Each box is called a pixel. Pictures that use straight lines are easy to make with pixels. Pictures that use curved or slanted lines are harder to draw.

Draw two different computer pictures below. Each little box stands for one pixel. You must color in the whole box or leave it blank. Try to draw a house, a tree, a face, or anything else you like. Before you begin, look at the different sizes of little boxes. Think about which picture would be best for each size.

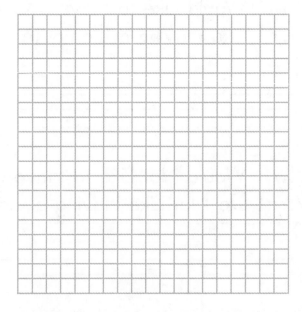

The Price is Right

Using coupons can sometimes help you buy things you want if you don't have enough money.

Pretend you want to buy these things:

milk	60¢	yo-yo	$1.50
cereal	$1.50	marker	80¢
toothpaste	$1.40	pad	70¢

You only have $1.00 to spend. But you have these coupons:

(continued)

MATHEMATICS ACTIVITY

The Price is Right

Use your coupons to figure out how much each thing will cost.
Then write the answers to the questions below.

What could you buy if you wanted to spend the whole dollar on one thing?

__toothpaste__   or   _____

What could you buy if you wanted to spend the whole dollar on two things?

_____   and   _____

(or)

_____   and   _____

30

PROBLEM SOLVING ACTIVITY

A Friend in Need

Imagine that the things below really happen. How could you help? Talk it over with a friend or family member. Write your ideas on the lines.

1. You find a puppy in your yard who looks lost.

2. Your friend is sick and can't come to school.

3. Your friend wants to buy his mother a birthday present, but he doesn't have any money.

4. Your little sister or brother starts crying when your parents leave you with the babysitter.

SOCIAL STUDIES ACTIVITY

All in the Family

A family tree can tell you if you or others in your family were named after parents or grandparents. Making a family tree is also a good way to learn more about who you are.

(continued)

SOCIAL STUDIES ACTIVITY

All in the Family

To make your family tree, draw a tree like the one on the previous page on a piece of poster board. Write your name and the names of your brothers and sisters on the trunk. On the first two branches, write the names of your parents. Go on up the tree with your parents' parents (your grandparents) and your grandparents' parents (your great-grandparents). Ask your parents or grandparents to tell you the names of your great-grandparents if they are not alive.

Make a leaf out of construction paper for each person on the tree. Find out the things listed on the leaf below. Write the information on the leaf. Then glue each leaf next to the person's place on your tree.

Share your tree with your family.

Great-grandmother
Louise Mary Smith
Born: May 10, 1901
Died: August 3, 1982
Children: William, Ann, Paul
Lived in: Little Rock,
    Arkansas
Job: Teacher

ART ACTIVITY

Greetings

Try making your own greeting cards.

You will need: construction paper, paints or markers, glue, felt, yarn

First, fold a piece of paper in four parts.

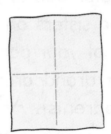 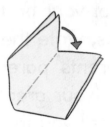

   On the outside, draw a picture and color it with paints or markers. You can also glue felt, yarn, or other things to your cover. On the inside, write your greeting.
   Many cards that you buy have poems for the greeting. Below are the first two lines of a poem for a birthday card and a poem for a thank-you card. Write two lines to finish each poem. Then use one of the poems to make a card.

On your birthday   The gift you gave
I just want to say,   Is what I wished for,

_____   _____

- - - - - - - - - - - - - - - -   - - - - - - - - - - - - - - - -

_____   _____

- - - - - - - - - - - - - - - -   - - - - - - - - - - - - - - - -

_____   _____

- - - - - - - - - - - - - - - -   - - - - - - - - - - - - - - - -

PROBLEM SOLVING ACTIVITY

Figure It Out!

Ice skaters whirl across the ice making circles, figure eights, loops, and spins. Here are two figures that they can skate.

Follow the arrows with your pencil to see how these figures are made on the ice.

Figure Eight

Double Loop Figure Eight

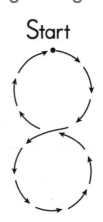

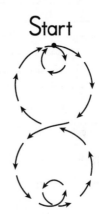

Try to copy each figure below *without lifting your pencil from the paper or going back over any line.*

1.

2.

3.

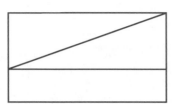

4.

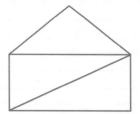

CREATIVE THINKING ACTIVITY

What Is It?

Can you think of some new ways to use the things below? Write your ideas on the lines. Then draw a picture showing one of your ideas for each thing.

an umbrella

_____

- -

_____

- -

_____

- -

a roller skate

_____

- -

_____

- -

_____

- -

a basket

_____

- -

_____

- -

_____

- -

CREATIVE THINKING ACTIVITY

Pass It On

Almost anyone you meet can teach you something. What might you learn from each of these people?

A passenger on a bus _____

_____

_____

_____

_____

A security guard _____

_____

_____

_____

_____

Your favorite movie star _____

_____

_____

_____

_____

CRITICAL THINKING ACTIVITY

Sorting It Out

Look at the animals below. How are they alike? Sort the animals by making groups for animals that are alike in some way. Write your reasons on the lines below.

deer

bear

rabbit

beaver

lizard

snake

parrot

pelican

Which animals are alike?

_____

_ _ _ _ _ _ _ _ _ _ _ _ _ _ _ _ _

_____

_ _ _ _ _ _ _ _ _ _ _ _ _ _ _ _ _

_____

_ _ _ _ _ _ _ _ _ _ _ _ _ _ _ _ _

_____

In what way are they alike?

_____

_ _ _ _ _ _ _ _ _ _ _ _ _ _ _ _ _

_____

_ _ _ _ _ _ _ _ _ _ _ _ _ _ _ _ _

_____

_ _ _ _ _ _ _ _ _ _ _ _ _ _ _ _ _

_____

CREATIVE THINKING ACTIVITY

Pick the Winner!

Choose your favorite story or your favorite character. Use words and pictures to make a medal for the winner. Then, on the lines, write why you liked the story or character best.

SCIENCE ACTIVITY

Don't Believe Everything You See

Sometimes your own eyes play tricks on you! Look at the pictures below and answer the questions.

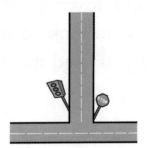

Is the witch's hat taller or wider? Really?

_____

_____

_____

Which street seems longer? Is it longer?

_____

_____

_____

Which block of cheese seems bigger? Is it?

_____

_____

_____

(continued)

SCIENCE ACTIVITY

Don't Believe Everything You See

Stare at the solid black dot for one minute. Then look at a blank piece of white paper. What do you see?

_____

- - - - - - - - - - - - - - - - - - - -

_____

- - - - - - - - - - - - - - - - - - - -

_____

- - - - - - - - - - - - - - - - - - - -

_____

Hole in the Hand

1. Roll a piece of paper into a tube.
2. Close your right eye.
3. Now hold the tube up to your left eye.
4. Look through the tube at something across the room.
5. Put your right hand next to the tube.
6. Now open your right eye. You will see your hand with a hole in it!

Out of This World

Use your imagination and take a trip into space.

What is the name of your spaceship? What does it look like? Write the name on the line. Then draw a picture of your spaceship in the box.

What things do you pass as you fly in space?

CRITICAL THINKING ACTIVITY

What Comes Next?

Look at these number patterns. What number comes next? Write the number in the blank.

5 10 15 20 25 30 35 40 45 _____

1 3 1 6 1 9 1 12 1 15 _____ _____ _____

Now figure out the picture patterns below. Draw a line to the picture that comes next in each pattern.

space capsule   rocket   flying saucer   flying wing   satellite   moon rover

SOCIAL STUDIES ACTIVITY

Soaring Solo

When pilots learn to fly, they use a compass. It helps them to know which way to fly. On the next page, put your pencil on START. Then follow the directions that tell you where to go next.

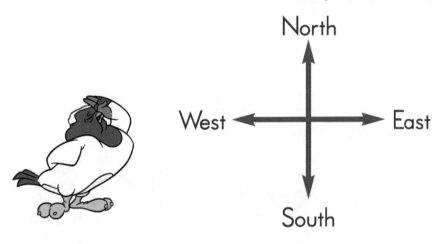

North

West ←——→ East

South

1. Go North 3 boxes.

2. Go East 3 boxes.

3. Go North 4 boxes.

4. Go East 2 boxes.

5. Go South 5 boxes.

6. Go East 5 boxes.

7. Go North 1 box.

8. Go East 1 box.

9. Go South 3 boxes.

10. Go West 1 box.

11. Go North 1 box.

12. Go West 5 boxes.

13. Go South 5 boxes.

14. Go West 2 boxes.

15. Go North 4 boxes.

16. Go West 3 boxes.

(continued)

SOCIAL STUDIES ACTIVITY

Soaring Solo

What shape do you see in the grid? Color it in.

Start •

SCIENCE ACTIVITY

Feel the Draft

Early balloons used heated air to lift them into the sky. The balloon rose because the hot air was lighter than the air outside the balloon. To see how hot air and cold air move, you can make a draft detector.

You will need

a thread spool   a paper clip
pencil (without a point)   paper
a paper straw   glue
a pin

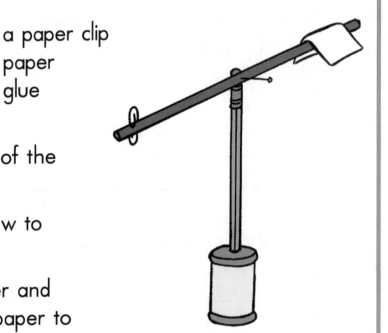

1. Put the pencil in the hole of the spool, eraser-end up.

2. Use a pin to hold the straw to the pencil eraser.

3. Cut a small piece of paper and bend it in half. Glue the paper to one end of the straw.

4. Put a paper clip on the other end of the straw. Move the clip or add another until the straw is balanced.

5. Now you are ready to try out your draft detector. Try it over a radiator or stove, near windows, or in front of an open refrigerator.

What happens? Does the hot air or the cold air lift the paper end? Which pushes it down?

CREATIVE THINKING ACTIVITY

What's That?

Below are some everyday things. List three new ways to use each of them. Your uses can be practical or silly. Then draw a picture to show your favorite idea.

A pillow

1.

2.

3.

A baseball cap

1.

2.

3.

A sock

1.

2.

3.

A tire

1.

2.

3.

SCIENCE ACTIVITY

The Ups and Downs of Air

A thermometer works a lot like a hot air or gas balloon. Make this model to see just how it works.

You Will Need

a small bottle   clay
food coloring   a clear plastic straw
water

1. Put a drop of food coloring into some water. Then put an inch of water into the bottle.

2. Place the straw into the bottle. The end should be in the water, but not touching the bottom.

3. Put the clay around the top of the bottle and the straw, so that air can't get out of the bottle.

4. Blow through the straw. When you take your mouth away, water should go up the straw. Blow a few more times until the water in the straw is about two inches above the clay.

Now, place your thermometer in ice-cold water. Watch it for a few minutes. Then put the bottle in hot water. What happens to the water in the bottle?

(continued)

SCIENCE ACTIVITY

The Ups and Downs of Air

When you put your thermometer in hot water, the air in the bottle heats up and expands. Since it needs more room, it pushes the water. The water has only one place to go—up the straw. Just the opposite happens as the temperature cools.

PROBLEM SOLVING ACTIVITY

Plane and Fancy

The Wright Brothers used kites to try out their ideas about flying. You can test your flying skills with a paper airplane. Here is one you can make.

1. Use an 8 1/2 inch by 11 inch piece of paper. Fold the paper in half the long way.

2. Open the paper. Now fold the two corners to make the nose of the plane. Make all your folds along the dotted lines.

3. Fold both corners again to the center.

4. Fold the ends once more to the center.

5. Turn the paper over. Bring the ends to the center and turn up the wings. Put a small piece of tape across the top to keep the wings together.

1.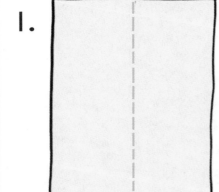

2.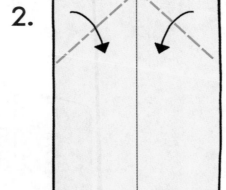

(continued)

NAME _____

PROBLEM SOLVING ACTIVITY

Plane and Fancy

3.
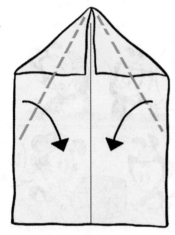

4.
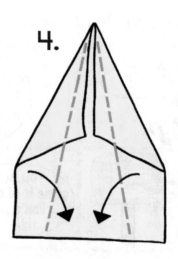

5.
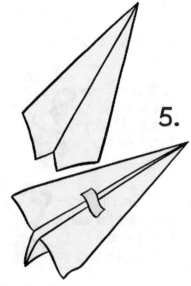

To fly your plane, point the nose down a little bit and push the plane forward to start it off. Try putting a paper clip on your plane, near the middle. How does it fly now? Move the clip and see what happens.

Do you want your plane to turn? Make two cuts on the back edge of each wing. To turn right, fold the left wing flap down. Now fold the right wing flap up. To make your plane fly to the left, fold the two flaps the opposite way.

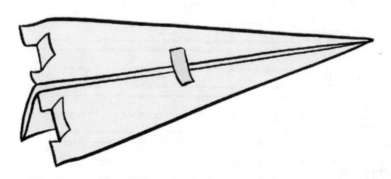

LANGUAGE ACTIVITY

What's the Word?

It's fun to make up new words. What do you think the made-up word in each cartoon means? Write your answers on the lines.

1. blechy _____

2. blarping _____

3. flutz _____

4. grinly _____

Now see if you can make up your own new words. Write a word for each meaning below.

1. Walking backwards _____

2. A pleasant smell _____

3. Very angry _____

4. A ruined dinner _____

52

PROBLEM SOLVING ACTIVITY

Crack That Code

People have been using codes to write secret messages for a very long time. Look at the messages below. Can you figure out what they say? (Hint: They both say the same thing!)

IHA VEAS ECRE THI DINGP LACE
ECALP GNIDIH TERCES A EVAH I

Did you figure out that the message says I HAVE A SECRET HIDING PLACE? In the first code, the spaces between words were changed. In the second, the message was written backwards.

Here is a more difficult code. Follow these directions to crack the coded messages below.

- Cross out the last letter of every word.
- Change every A to E. Change every E to A.
- Change every I to O. Change every O to I.

1. MAATH MAX ETS MYL HIUSAN.

   Meet me at my house.

2. LIIKP OND THAP SHADY IUTR BECKD.

   _____

3. OL WOLLK BAH WEOTONGZ FIRC YIUF.

   _____

CRITICAL THINKING ACTIVITY

THINK

On Schedule

Dr. Scratchansniff does the same things every morning at exactly the same times. If Dr. Scratchansniff kept a log of his schedule, it might look something like this:

MY SCHEDULE	
7:00	Wake up, look for glasses.
7:15	Find glasses, make bed, get dressed, polish head to a pretty shine.
7:50	Leave for studio.
8:10	Hide lunch from Wakko Warner.
12:00	Lock door, eat lunch under desk.
5:00	Escape from studio.

Making a schedule can help you keep track of all the things you have to do. It can also help you use your time wisely. First, make a list of everything you have to do each day. Include meals, school, afterschool activities, chores, and homework. Then write down the times you do each thing. If your schedule changes from day to day, write down the day next to the activity. Then organize your list into a schedule like the one started below.

MY SCHEDULE	
7:00	Get up, make bed, dress
7:45	Eat breakfast, take out garbage
8:30	Leave for school
3:30	Arrive home from school

ART ACTIVITY

Make A Face

You can tell a lot about how a person is feeling just by the look on his or her face. Drawings of faces can show feelings, too. Look at the simple face drawings below. On the line under each picture, write a word to describe each expression.

happy

Now draw your own faces in the circles below. You might try these expressions: bored, worried, laughing. It helps to feel the expression you are trying to draw. So, make faces while you are drawing faces! Label each drawing with a word that describes the expression.

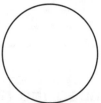

SOCIAL STUDIES ACTIVITY

On the Trail

Symbols on a map can help you find things. Use the map and the map key to answer the questions below.

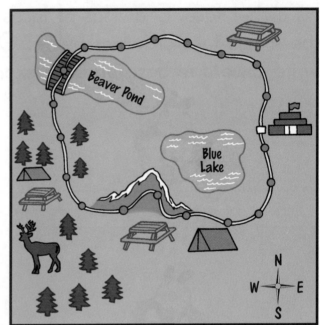

KEY

- Hiking Trail
- Visitor's Center
- Body of Water
- Forest
- Camping Area
- Picnic Area
- Bridge
- Hill
- Deer Trail

1. Where does the hiking trail begin and end?

    At the Visitor's Center

2. How many camping areas are show on the map? _____

3. Over what body of water is there a bridge? _____

4. Is the forest east or west of Blue Lake? _____

5. The hikers stopped for a picnic after they climbed the hill. Put a circle around the symbol that shows where they stopped.

56

PROBLEM SOLVING ACTIVITY

It's A-Maze-Ing

See how quickly you can get to the center of the maze below. Use a pencil to mark the trail.

ENTER

CREATIVE THINKING ACTIVITY

Knock, Knock!

A knock-knock joke is a kind of joke that is fun and easy to tell. See if you can finish the knock-knock jokes below. Use your imagination! Then tell your favorite ones to a friend.

1. Knock, knock.
   Who's there?
   Yule.
   Yule who?

   Yule miss me
   when I'm gone.

2. Knock, knock.
   Who's there?
   Will.
   Will who?

3. Knock, knock.
   Who's there?
   Otto.
   Otto who?

4. Knock, knock.
   Who's there?
   Eileen.
   Eileen who?

5. Knock, knock.
   Who's there?
   Wanda.
   Wanda who?

6. Knock, knock.
   Who's there?
   Linda.
   Linda who?

CRITICAL THINKING ACTIVITY

What Does the Sign Say?

In many places there are signs to warn us of danger, to tell us about laws that must be obeyed, or to give us other information.

Some signs have pictures, or symbols, instead of words. The symbols are easy for people to read at a glance.

Figure out what each sign means. Write each meaning on the lines.

1. No Bicycles

2. _____

3. _____

4. _____

Draw a sign for each item below. Be sure your signs are easy to understand.

5. HIKING TRAIL

6. NO DOGS ALLOWED

CRITICAL THINKING ACTIVITY

On the Right Track

One of the secrets of a wildlife watcher is learning how to identify animal tracks.

Look at the drawings of each animal's feet and the sample set of tracks. Then use the clues below to identify which animal made each track. Write the name of the animal on the line under each track.

1. dog

2. _____

3. _____

4. _____

5. _____

1. Dog and cat tracks look a lot alike. Both show only four toes and have almost the same shaped heel pad. But a cat's tracks don't show toenails or claws. Also, a line of cat tracks is usually straighter than the trail left by a dog.

2. Like many birds, sparrows and pigeons have three toes in the front and one behind. The bird that spends most of its time on the ground walks just like you do. The bird that lives mostly in trees hops when it is on the ground.

3. The squirrel is a hopping animal. It has sharp claws on all toes to help it climb trees. Like most animals that walk flat-footed, it has larger hind feet than forefeet.

LANGUAGE ACTIVITY

A Way with Words

When two things are compared using the word like or as, it is called a simile. Similes help readers to see and feel what is being described.

You can create similes, too. Combine a phrase from the list on the left with a word or phrase from the list on the right. Write your similes on the lines below.

I was as quiet as a	a drill.
Its fur was as soft as	a lark.
It shook like	a mouse.
It ran as fast as	stars.
It had eyes as happy as	silk.
I felt as happy as	a jet.

I was as quiet as a mouse.

_____

_____

_____

_____

_____

_____

_____

_____

Choose three of the similes you wrote and use them in a paragraph. Write a description of something you might see in the woods. Write your paragraph on another piece of paper.

SCIENCE ACTIVITY

Seeing Seashells

You can learn to identify shells. Many shells are named for the way they look. Look for clues in the names of the shells listed on the next page to match the name with the right picture. Write the name of the shell on the line under each picture.

1. Top Shell

2. _____

3. _____

4. _____

5. _____

6. _____

(continued)

SCIENCE ACTIVITY

Olive Shell	Heart Cockle	Worm Shell
Top Shell	Angel Wing	Moon Shell
Tusk Shell	Slipper Shell	Volcano Limpet
Panther Cowrie	Spider Conch	Cone Shell

7. _____

8. _____

9. _____

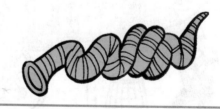

10. _____

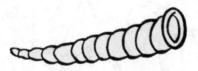

11. _____

12. _____

CRITICAL THINKING ACTIVITY

Are You a Good Detective?

How are your "seeing" powers? There are eight things wrong in the picture below. Can you detect all of them?

ANSWER KEY

MATHEMATICS ACTIVITY

Find the Objects

Find and count the benches, kites, pigeons, and dogs in the picture. Write the numbers on the lines.

2 benches   5 dogs

8 pigeons   3 kites

3

LANGUAGE ACTIVITY

Sentence Mix-Ups

Unscramble the words in each group to make a sentence. The first word in each sentence is in the right place. Write each sentence on the lines.

1. My checkup today is.

   My checkup is today.

2. The my takes pulse nurse.

   The nurse takes my pulse.

3. I getting like shots don't.

   I don't like getting shots.

4. A reward a good is candy bar.

   A candy bar is a good reward.

4

LANGUAGE ACTIVITY

Make a Word   Answers may vary.

Draw a line from the sidecar to each motorcycle to complete a word.

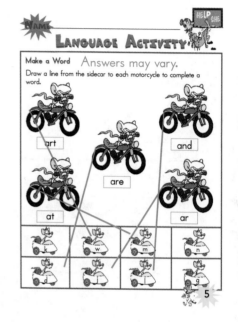

5

MATHEMATICS ACTIVITY

By the Sea

Find out how many of each animal are in the sea.

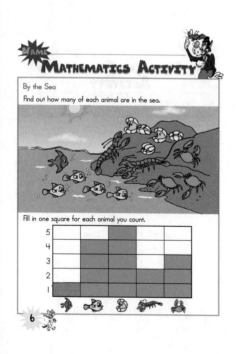

Fill in one square for each animal you count.

6

PROBLEM SOLVING ACTIVITY

Go Home

Use your finger to trace a path through the maze to connect The Brain to the lab. Then use a green crayon to mark the path. Use a different colored crayon for the paths of each of the other characters.

Can you help The Brain go to the (lab)?

Can you help Slappy get to her (treehouse)?

Can you help Dot get to the (water tower)?

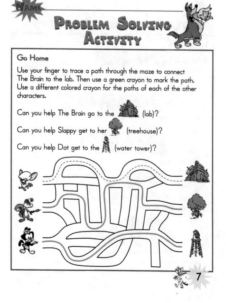

7

CRITICAL THINKING ACTIVITY

What Is In It?

Identify each object on the left and determine which object in the row would most logically be inside. Circle your choices.

8

65

ANSWER KEY

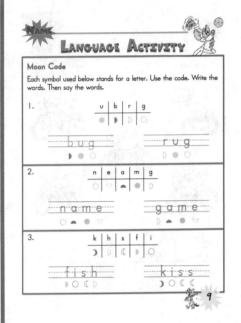

LANGUAGE ACTIVITY

Moon Code

Each symbol used below stands for a letter. Use the code. Write the words. Then say the words.

1. | u | b | r | g |

   b u g   r u g

2. | n | e | a | m | g |

   n a m e   g a m e

3. | k | h | s | f | i |

   f i s h   k i s s

9

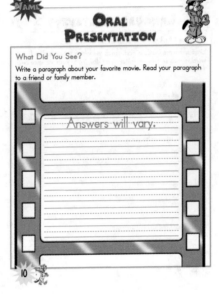

ORAL PRESENTATION

What Did You See?

Write a paragraph about your favorite movie. Read your paragraph to a friend or family member.

Answers will vary.

10

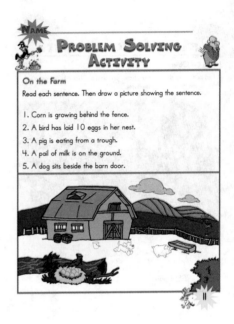

PROBLEM SOLVING ACTIVITY

On the Farm

Read each sentence. Then draw a picture showing the sentence.

1. Corn is growing behind the fence.
2. A bird has laid 10 eggs in her nest.
3. A pig is eating from a trough.
4. A pail of milk is on the ground.
5. A dog sits beside the barn door.

11

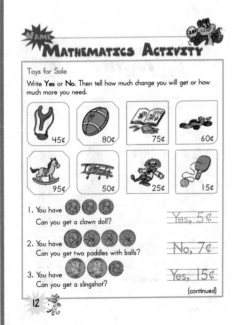

MATHEMATICS ACTIVITY

Toys for Sale

Write **Yes** or **No**. Then tell how much change you will get or how much more you need.

45¢   80¢   75¢   60¢

95¢   50¢   25¢   15¢

1. You have
   Can you get a clown doll?   Yes, 5¢

2. You have
   Can you get two paddles with balls?   No, 7¢

3. You have
   Can you get a slingshot?   Yes, 15¢

(continued)

12

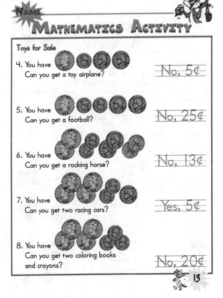

MATHEMATICS ACTIVITY

Toys for Sale

4. You have
   Can you get a toy airplane?   No, 5¢

5. You have
   Can you get a football?   No, 25¢

6. You have
   Can you get a rocking horse?   No, 13¢

7. You have
   Can you get two racing cars?   Yes, 5¢

8. You have
   Can you get two coloring books
   and crayons?   No, 20¢

13

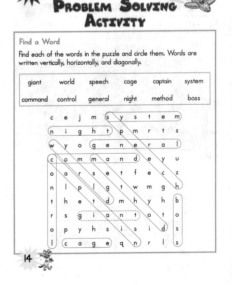

PROBLEM SOLVING ACTIVITY

Find a Word

Find each of the words in the puzzle and circle them. Words are written vertically, horizontally, and diagonally.

| giant | world | speech | cage | captain | system |
| command | control | general | night | method | boss |

```
c e j m s y s t e m
n i g h t p m r t s
w y o g e n e r a l
c o m m a n d e y u
o a r s e t f e c z
n l p l g t w m g h
t h e t d m h y h b
r s g i a n t o t o
o p y h s i s i d s
l c a g e q n r l l
```

14

66

ANSWER KEY

LANGUAGE ACTIVITY

What Is My Name?

Each letter of the alphabet has a symbol. Use the code to make names. Write the names.

A	B	C	D	E	F	G	H	I
○	□	△	☆	⋏	⊞	⊙	◇	☺

J	K	L	M	N	O	P	Q	R
◧	⬧	▽	▭	✚	✕	⋈	◑	♡

S	T	U	V	W	X	Y	Z
⊕	◎	⊡	▽	⊠	⎯	⬆	⬇

Plotz
⋈ ▽ ○ ◎ ⬇

Marita
▭ ○ ♡ ☺ ◎ ○

Flavio
⊞ ▽ ○ ▽ ☺ ✕

Pinky
⋈ ☺ ✚ ⬧ ⬆

Write your name in code. _Answers will vary._

15

LANGUAGE ACTIVITY

Crack the Code

There are many different kinds of codes. Crack each coded message below. Read the clues to help you.

1. REWOT RETAW EHT TA EM TEEM
   Clue: This message is written backwards.

   Meet me at the water tower.

2. WEA RAC LEV ERD ISG UIS E
   Clue: The spaces between the words are in the wrong place.

   Wear a clever disguise.

3. EP OPU XBLF VQ UIF HVBSE
   Clue: Change each letter to the one that comes before it in the alphabet.

   Do not wake up the guard.

4. 8-5 23-9-12-12 2-5 13-1-4
   Clue: The number 1 stands for A, 2 stands for B, and so on. Write the alphabet under the numbers 1-26.

   He will be mad.

Use these codes to write your own secret messages to a friend. Then make up your own codes to share.

16

RESEARCH AND REPORTING ACTIVITY

Tell All About It

You know that a library has many kinds of books. It has story books, books that give information, and books about real people.

Go to the library and read a book of your choice. You can ask the librarian to help you pick out a book. Tell the librarian what kind of book you would like to read.

Fill out the form below to tell about your book.

Title _____ Answers will vary.

Author _____

Kind of Book _____

What the Book is About _____

My Favorite Part _____

17

CRITICAL THINKING ACTIVITY

The Name Game

Work with a friend to make a name book.

First write down all the letters, A to Z. Then think of all the names you know that begin with A. Go on to B, C, and all the others.

Count up all the names for each letter. Color in one box for each name.

Answers will vary.

A B C D E F G H I J K L M

N O P Q R S T U V W X Y Z

What letters have the most names? Is there a letter with no names? How many names begin with the same letter as yours?

Ask your family to tell you why they gave you your name. Tell the story to your friends.

18

CREATIVE THINKING ACTIVITY

Who Am I?

Here is a guessing game you can play in a group. The name of the game is "What's My Name?"

One player thinks of a person everyone knows. It can be a real person, or it can be a character from a book, movie, or television show.

Then the player gives a few clues to help the others guess the name. Can you guess the name from the clues below?

Abraham Lincoln

My face is in a monument.
I had a beard and wore a tall hat.
I was a president.
I was very honest.

The other players take turns guessing. If no one can guess, the players can ask for another clue. The first player to say the right name gets to be the next mystery person.

19

CRITICAL THINKING ACTIVITY

Which Is It?

Look at these cakes. They all look the same, don't they? One cake is different. Look again, closely. Find the cake that is different. Then circle the two things that make it different.

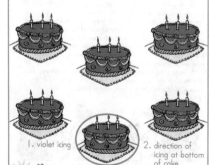

 1. violet icing

 2. direction of icing at bottom of cake

20

67

ANSWER KEY

Name

LANGUAGE ACTIVITY

Picture This

Did you know that you can write messages using pictures? A *rebus* is a kind of puzzle that uses pictures for words. Can you figure out what each rebus below says? Write the word under each picture.

ch + [ear] → cheer   [eye][ball] → eyeball   [bee][knee] + th → beneath

Now write what this rebus says.

Buttons saw Mindy in a tree. Buttons tried
to bring Mindy down. Mindy would rather
sit there. Buttons will go home.

Try to make your own rebus. Leave spaces between the words. Use a + sign to link sounds that make one word. Give your rebus to a friend to figure out.

21

Name

ART ACTIVITY

Swimming Fish

Mobiles are kinds of art work that can move in the wind. You can make your own mobile of fish swimming.

You Will Need

colored construction paper   thread
scissors   a wire hanger

1. First make six fish using different colored construction paper. Fold a piece of paper in half. Cut along the dotted lines as shown in the picture. Open up your paper and you have a fish! Draw a mouth and an eye on each side of your fish.

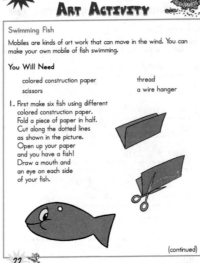

(continued)

22

Name

ART ACTIVITY

Swimming Fish

2. Cut a long piece of thread. Use a pencil to make a hole in each fish. Move the point around until the hole is big enough for the thread. Put one end through the hole and tie a knot. Be careful not to tie your finger—you're way too heavy for the mobile.

3. Now it is time to put your mobile together. Tie each fish to the wire hanger. Before you make knots, hold up the hanger and see if your mobile is balanced. You can pull on the thread to make the fish hang longer or shorter. You can also move the thread from side to side. Move your fish until your mobile is balanced. Then tie a knot to keep each fish in place.

4. Hang up your mobile in a place where there is a little breeze so you can watch your fish swim!

23

Name

SCIENCE ACTIVITY

Just Tasting

Sometimes you use different senses at the same time. Do you think you use only your sense of taste when you eat? Here is a way you can find out.

You will need some bite-sized pieces of food that are all crunchy, like an apple, carrot, turnip, and raw potato. You can try creamy things, too—ice cream, pudding, yogurt, and mashed potatoes.

This is an activity for you to do with one or more friends. One of you needs to cover your eyes with a cloth and hold your nose. Someone puts a piece of one of the foods in your mouth. You try to guess what it is. Take turns so each of you gets a chance to test your tasting sense. Write down which foods were the hardest to guess.

Try this with things you drink, too. See if anyone can guess which is orange juice and which is grapefruit juice. Make sure you cover your eyes and hold your nose.

What does this tell you about tasting? Do you use only your sense of taste when you eat, or are other senses important, too? Is your sense of taste linked more to your sight or smell?

24

Name

MATHEMATICS ACTIVITY

Making Change

You can practice making change with a friend or family member by playing the game below.

You Will Need: cardboard, scissors

First, make coins by cutting out circles for pennies, nickels, dimes, and quarters. Write 1¢, 5¢, 10¢, or 25¢ on each coin. Each of you should have ten pennies, five nickels, three dimes, and two quarters.

To play, one of you starts by making up a problem, such as this one:

   I bought something that cost 33 cents.
   I gave the salesman one quarter and one dime.
   How much change did I get?

As you say the problem, show your partner the coins you used. Your partner has to add up the coins and make the right change. Did you figure out that the answer to this problem is two cents change?

Take turns giving problems and making change. Each time you make the right change, you get one point. The player with the most points wins the game.

25

Name

SOCIAL STUDIES ACTIVITY

Wave the Flag

The flag of the United States has 13 stripes and 50 stars. The 13 stripes stand for the first 13 states. The 50 stars stand for the 50 states we have today. Did you know that every country in the world has its own flag?

Use an information book in the library to help you find a picture of a flag from another country. Draw the flag in the box. Write the name of the country on the line.

Answers will vary.

Did you know that every state also has its own flag? Find a picture of your state flag and draw it in the box. Write the name of your state on the line.

Even your school can have a flag! Make up a flag for your school and draw it in the box. Write the name of your school on the line.

26

ANSWER KEY

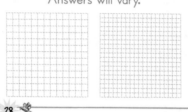

CRITICAL THINKING ACTIVITY

What Do You Think?

Pretend that your family is thinking about buying a computer. Think of reasons why you would like to have a computer. What would you use a computer for? Taking over the world? Keeping track of Pinky's thoughts? How would other people in your family use the computer? If you already have a computer, think about why you like having one.

Also think of reasons why you might not like to have a computer. Would the computer be hard to share? Would the computer take too much time away from doing other things? If you already have a computer, are there any things you do not like about it?

Write down your reasons on the lines below. Use another sheet of paper if you need to.

Why I Would Like to Have a Computer (or)
Why I Like Having a Computer
_____ Answers will vary. _____

Why I Would Not Like to Have a Computer (or)
Why I Do Not Like Having a Computer

27

CREATIVE THINKING ACTIVITY

Box by Box

Drawing on a computer is not the same as drawing on paper. The pictures that you see on a computer are made up of hundreds of little boxes. Each box is called a pixel. Pictures that use straight lines are easy to make with pixels. Pictures that use curved or slanted lines are harder to draw.

Draw two different computer pictures below. Each little box stands for one pixel. You must color in the whole box or leave it blank. Try to draw a house, a tree, a face, or anything else you like. Before you begin, look at the different sizes of little boxes. Think about which picture would be best for each size.

Answers will vary.

28

MATHEMATICS ACTIVITY

The Price is Right

Using coupons can sometimes help you buy things you want if you don't have enough money.

Pretend you want to buy these things:

milk	60¢	yo-yo	$1.50
cereal	$1.50	marker	80¢
toothpaste	$1.40	pad	70¢

You only have $1.00 to spend. But you have these coupons:

10¢ OFF	$1.00 OFF	40¢ OFF
50¢ OFF	20¢ OFF	30¢ OFF

(continued)

29

MATHEMATICS ACTIVITY

The Price is Right

Use your coupons to figure out how much each thing will cost. Then write the answers to the questions below.

What could you buy if you wanted to spend the whole dollar on one thing?

_____ toothpaste _____ or _____ yo-yo _____

What could you buy if you wanted to spend the whole dollar on two things?

_____ milk _____ and _____ cereal _____

(or)

_____ marker _____ and _____ pad _____

30

PROBLEM SOLVING ACTIVITY

A Friend in Need

Imagine that the things below really happen. How could you help? Talk it over with a friend or family member. Write your ideas on the lines.

1. You find a puppy in your yard who looks lost.
_____ Answers will vary. _____

2. Your friend is sick and can't come to school.

3. Your friend wants to buy his mother a birthday present, but he doesn't have any money.

4. Your little sister or brother starts crying when your parents leave you with the babysitter.

31

SOCIAL STUDIES ACTIVITY

All in the Family

A family tree can tell you if you or others in your family were named after parents or grandparents. Making a family tree is also a good way to learn more about who you are.

(continued)

32

ANSWER KEY

SOCIAL STUDIES ACTIVITY

All in the Family

To make your family tree, draw a tree like the one on the previous page on a piece of poster board. Write your name and the names of your brothers and sisters on the trunk. On the first two branches, write the names of your parents. Go on up the tree with your parents' parents (your grandparents) and your grandparents' parents (your great-grandparents). Ask your parents or grandparents to tell you the names of your great-grandparents if they are not alive.

Make a leaf out of construction paper for each person on the tree. Find out the things listed on the leaf below. Write the information on the leaf. Then glue each leaf next to the person's place on your tree.

Share your tree with your family.

> Great-grandmother
> Louise Mary Smith
> Born: May 10, 1901
> Died: August 3, 1982
> Children: William, Ann, Paul
> Lived in: Little Rock, Arkansas
> Job: Teacher

33

ART ACTIVITY

Greetings

Try making your own greeting cards.

You will need: construction paper, paints or markers, glue, felt, yarn

First, fold a piece of paper in four parts.

On the outside, draw a picture and color it with paints or markers. You can also glue felt, yarn, or other things to your cover. On the inside, write your greeting.

Many cards that you buy have poems for the greeting. Below are the first two lines of a poem for a birthday card and a poem for a thank-you card. Write two lines to finish each poem. Then use one of the poems to make a card.

On your birthday I just want to say,	The gift you gave Is what I wished for,
Answers will vary.	

34

PROBLEM SOLVING ACTIVITY

Figure It Out!

Ice skaters whirl across the ice making circles, figure eights, loops, and spins. Here are two figures that they can skate.

Follow the arrows with your pencil to see how these figures are made on the ice.

Figure Eight — Start

Double Loop Figure Eight — Start

Try to copy each figure below *without lifting your pencil from the paper or going back over any line.*

1.   2.   3.   4.

35

CREATIVE THINKING ACTIVITY

What Is It?

Can you think of some new ways to use the things below? Write your ideas on the lines. Then draw a picture showing one of your ideas for each thing.

an umbrella

Answers will vary.

a roller skate

a basket

36

CREATIVE THINKING ACTIVITY

Pass It On

Almost anyone you meet can teach you something. What might you learn from each of these people?

A passenger on a bus    Answers will vary.

A security guard

Your favorite movie star

37

CRITICAL THINKING ACTIVITY

Sorting It Out

Look at the animals below. How are they alike? Sort the animals by making groups for animals that are alike in some way. Write your reasons on the lines below.

deer	bear	rabbit	beaver
lizard	snake	parrot	pelican

Which animals are alike?	In what way are they alike?
	Answers will vary.

38

70

ANSWER KEY

CREATIVE THINKING ACTIVITY

Pick the Winner!

Choose your favorite story or your favorite character. Use words and pictures to make a medal for the winner. Then, on the lines, write why you liked the story or character best.

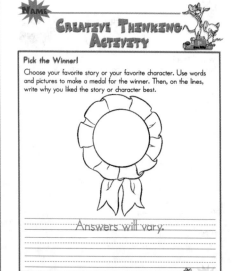

Answers will vary.

39

SCIENCE ACTIVITY

Don't Believe Everything You See

Sometimes your own eyes play tricks on you! Look at the pictures below and answer the questions.

Is the witch's hat taller or wider? Really?

The hat looks taller, but the height and length are the same measure.

Which street seems longer? Is it longer?

The vertical street seems longer, but both streets are the same length.

Which block of cheese seems bigger? Is it?

The block of cheese on the left seems bigger, but both blocks are the same size.

(continued)

40

SCIENCE ACTIVITY

Don't Believe Everything You See

Stare at the solid black dot for one minute. Then look at a blank piece of white paper. What do you see?

You should see the black dot.

Hole in the Hand
1. Roll a piece of paper into a tube.
2. Close your right eye.
3. Now hold the tube up to your left eye.
4. Look through the tube at something across the room.
5. Put your right hand next to the tube.
6. Now open your right eye. You will see your hand with a hole in it!

41

DRAMA ACTIVITY

Out of This World

Use your imagination and take a trip into space.

What is the name of your spaceship? What does it look like? Write the name on the line. Then draw a picture of your spaceship in the box.

Answers will vary.

What things do you pass as you fly in space?

Answers will vary.

42

CRITICAL THINKING ACTIVITY

What Comes Next?

Look at these number patterns. What number comes next? Write the number in the blank.

5 10 15 20 25 30 35   40 45   50

1 3 6 1 9 1 12 1 15   1   18   1

Now figure out the picture patterns below. Draw a line to the picture that comes next in each pattern.

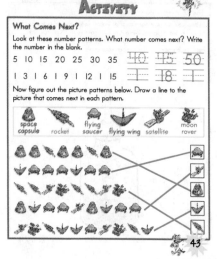

space capsule rocket flying saucer flying wing satellite moon rover

43

SOCIAL STUDIES ACTIVITY

Soaring Solo

When pilots learn to fly, they use a compass. It helps them to know which way to fly. On the next page, put your pencil on START. Then follow the directions that tell you where to go next.

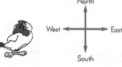

North
West ← → East
South

1. Go North 3 boxes.
2. Go East 3 boxes.
3. Go North 4 boxes.
4. Go East 2 boxes.
5. Go South 5 boxes.
6. Go East 5 boxes.
7. Go North 1 box.
8. Go East 1 box.
9. Go South 3 boxes.
10. Go West 1 box.
11. Go North 1 box.
12. Go West 5 boxes.
13. Go South 5 boxes.
14. Go West 2 boxes.
15. Go North 4 boxes.
16. Go West 3 boxes.

(continued)

44

ANSWER KEY

SOCIAL STUDIES ACTIVITY

Soaring Solo

What shape do you see in the grid? Color it in.

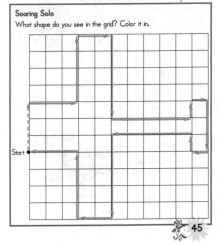

Start

45

SCIENCE ACTIVITY

Feel the Draft

Early balloons used heated air to lift them into the sky. The balloon rose because the hot air was lighter than the air outside the balloon. To see how hot air and cold air move, you can make a draft detector.

You will need

a thread spool   a paper clip
pencil (without a point)   paper
a paper straw   glue
a pin

1. Put the pencil in the hole of the spool, eraser-end up.

2. Use a pin to hold the straw to the pencil eraser.

3. Cut a small piece of paper and bend it in half. Glue the paper to one end of the straw.

4. Put a paper clip on the other end of the straw. Move the clip or add another until the straw is balanced.

5. Now you are ready to try out your draft detector. Try it over a radiator or stove, near windows, or in front of an open refrigerator.

What happens? Does the hot air or the cold air lift the paper end? Which pushes it down?

46

CREATIVE THINKING ACTIVITY

What's That?

Below are some everyday things. List three new ways to use each of them. Your uses can be practical or silly. Then draw a picture to show your favorite idea.

A pillow

1. Answers will vary.
2.
3.

A baseball cap

1.
2.
3.

A sock

1.
2.
3.

A tire

1.
2.
3.

47

SCIENCE ACTIVITY

The Ups and Downs of Air

A thermometer works a lot like a hot air or gas balloon. Make this model to see just how it works.

You Will Need

a small bottle   clay
food coloring   a clear plastic straw
water

1. Put a drop of food coloring into some water. Then put an inch of water into the bottle.

2. Place the straw into the bottle. The end should be in the water, but not touching the bottom.

3. Put the clay around the top of the bottle and the straw, so that air can't get out of the bottle.

4. Blow through the straw. When you take your mouth away, water should go up the straw. Blow a few more times until the water in the straw is about two inches above the clay.

Now, place your thermometer in ice-cold water. Watch it for a few minutes. Then put the bottle in hot water. What happens to the water in the bottle?

(continued)

48

SCIENCE ACTIVITY

The Ups and Downs of Air

When you put your thermometer in hot water, the air in the bottle heats up and expands. Since it needs more room, it pushes the water. The water has only one place to go—up the straw. Just the opposite happens as the temperature cools.

49

PROBLEM SOLVING ACTIVITY

Plane and Fancy

The Wright Brothers used kites to try out their ideas about flying. You can test your flying skills with a paper airplane. Here is one you can make.

1. Use an 8 1/2 inch by 11 inch piece of paper. Fold the paper in half the long way.

2. Open the paper. Now fold the two corners to make the nose of the plane. Make all your folds along the dotted lines.

3. Fold both corners again to the center.

4. Fold the ends once more to the center.

5. Turn the paper over. Bring the ends to the center and turn up the wings. Put a small piece of tape across the top to keep the wings together.

1.   2.

(continued)

50

ANSWER KEY

PROBLEM SOLVING ACTIVITY

Plane and Fancy

3.   4.   5.

To fly your plane, point the nose down a little bit and push the plane forward to start it off. Try putting a paper clip on your plane, near the middle. How does it fly now? Move the clip and see what happens.

Do you want your plane to turn? Make two cuts on the back edge of each wing. To turn right, fold the left wing flap down. Now fold the right wing flap up. To make your plane fly to the left, fold the two flaps the opposite way.

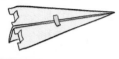

51

LANGUAGE ACTIVITY

What's the Word?

It's fun to make up new words. What do you think the made-up word in each cartoon means? Write your answers on the lines.

1. blechy _____Answers will vary._____

2. blarping _____

3. flutz _____

4. grinly _____

Now see if you can make up your own new words. Write a word for each meaning below.

1. Walking backwards _____Answers will vary._____

2. A pleasant smell _____

3. Very angry _____

4. A ruined dinner _____

52

PROBLEM SOLVING ACTIVITY

Crack That Code

People have been using codes to write secret messages for a very long time. Look at the messages below. Can you figure out what they say? (Hint: They both say the same thing!)

IHA VEAS ECRE THI DIINGP LACE
ECALP GNIDIH TERCES A EVAH I

Did you figure out that the message says I HAVE A SECRET HIDING PLACE? In the first code, the spaces between words were changed. In the second, the message was written backwards.

Here is a more difficult code. Follow these directions to crack the coded messages below.

- Cross out the last letter of every word.
- Change every A to E. Change every E to A.
- Change every I to O. Change every O to I.

1. MAATH MAX ETS MYL HIUSAN.
   _____Meet me at my house._____

2. LIIKP OND THAP SHADY IUTR BECKD.
   _____Look in the shed out back._____

3. OL WOLLK BAH WEOTONGZ FIRC YIUE
   _____I will be waiting for you._____

53

CRITICAL THINKING ACTIVITY

On Schedule

Dr. Scratchansniff does the same things every morning at exactly the same times. If Dr. Scratchansniff kept a log of his schedule, it might look something like this:

MY SCHEDULE	
7:00	Wake up, look for glasses.
7:15	Find glasses, make bed, get dressed, polish head to a pretty shine.
7:50	Leave for studio.
8:10	Hide lunch from Wakko Warner.
12:00	Lock door, eat lunch under desk.
5:00	Escape from studio.

Making a schedule can help you keep track of all the things you have to do. It can also help you use your time wisely. First, make a list of everything you have to do each day. Include meals, school, afterschool activities, chores, and homework. Then write down the times you do each thing. If your schedule changes from day to day, write down the day next to the activity. Then organize your list into a schedule like the one started below.

MY SCHEDULE	
7:00	Get up, make bed, dress
7:45	Eat breakfast, take out garbage
8:30	Leave for school
3:30	Arrive home from school

54

ART ACTIVITY

Make A Face

You can tell a lot about how a person is feeling just by the look on his or her face. Drawings of faces can show feelings, too. Look at the simple face drawings below. On the line under each picture, write a word to describe each expression.

_____happy_____   _____sad_____

_____angry_____   _____surprised_____

Now draw your own faces in the circles below. You might try these expressions: bored, worried, laughing. It helps to feel the expression you are trying to draw. So, make faces while you are drawing faces! Label each drawing with a word that describes the expression.

_____Answers will vary._____

55

SOCIAL STUDIES ACTIVITY

On the Trail

Symbols on a map can help you find things. Use the map and the map key to answer the questions below.

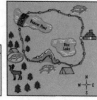

KEY		
Hiking Trail		Picnic Area
Visitor's Center		Bridge
Body of Water		Hill
Forest		Deer Trail
Camping Area		

1. Where does the hiking trail begin and end?
   _____At the Visitor's Center_____

2. How many camping areas are show on the map? _____2_____

3. Over what body of water is there a bridge? _____Beaver Pond_____

4. Is the forest east or west of Blue Lake? _____west_____

5. The hikers stopped for a picnic after they climbed the hill. Put a circle around the symbol that shows where they stopped.

56

Answer Key

Problem Solving Activity

It's A-Maze-Ing

See how quickly you can get to the center of the maze below. Use a pencil to mark the trail.

ENTER

57

Creative Thinking Activity

Knock, Knock!

A knock-knock joke is a kind of joke that is fun and easy to tell. See if you can finish the knock-knock jokes below. Use your imagination! Then tell your favorite ones to a friend.

1. Knock, knock.
Who's there?
Yule.
Yule who?
Yule miss me
when I'm gone.

2. Knock, knock.
Who's there?
Will.
Will who?
Answers will
vary.

3. Knock, knock.
Who's there?
Otto.
Otto who?
_____

4. Knock, knock.
Who's there?
Eileen.
Eileen who?
_____

5. Knock, knock.
Who's there?
Wanda.
Wanda who?
_____

6. Knock, knock.
Who's there?
Linda.
Linda who?
_____

58

Critical Thinking Activity

What Does the Sign Say?

In many places there are signs to warn us of danger, to tell us about laws that must be obeyed, or to give us other information.

Some signs have pictures, or symbols, instead of words. The symbols are easy for people to read at a glance.

Figure out what each sign means. Write each meaning on the lines.

1. No Bicycles   2. Steep Hill

3. School Crossing   4. Gas Station

Draw a sign for each item below. Be sure your signs are easy to understand.

5. HIKING TRAIL   6. NO DOGS ALLOWED

59

Critical Thinking Activity

On the Right Track

One of the secrets of a wildlife watcher is learning how to identify animal tracks.

Look at the drawings of each animal's feet and the sample set of tracks. Then use the clues below to identify which animal made each track. Write the name of the animal on the line under each track.

1. dog   2. pigeon   3. cat

4. squirrel   5. sparrow

1. Dog and cat tracks look a lot alike. Both show only four toes and have almost the same shaped heel pad. But a cat's tracks don't show toenails or claws. Also, a line of cat tracks is usually straighter than the trail left by a dog.
2. Like many birds, sparrows and pigeons have three toes in the front and one behind. The bird that spends most of its time on the ground walks just like you do. The bird that lives mostly in trees hops when it is on the ground.
3. The squirrel is a hopping animal. It has sharp claws on all toes to help it climb trees. Like most animals that walk flat-footed, it has larger hind feet than forefeet.

60

Language Activity

A Way with Words

When two things are compared using the word like or as, it is called a simile. Similes help readers to see and feel what is being described.

You can create similes, too. Combine a phrase from the list on the left with a word or phrase from the list on the right. Write your similes on the lines below.

I was as quiet as a	a drill.
Its fur was as soft as	a lark.
It shook like	a mouse.
It ran as fast as	a jet.
It had eyes as happy as	stars.
I felt as happy as	silk.

I was as quiet as a mouse.

Its fur was as soft as silk.

It shook like a drill.

It ran as fast as a jet.

It had eyes like stars.

I felt as happy as a lark.

Choose three of the similes you wrote and use them in a paragraph. Write a description of something you might see in the woods. Write your paragraph on another piece of paper.

Answers will vary.

61

Science Activity

Seeing Seashells

You can learn to identify shells. Many shells are named for the way they look. Look for clues in the names of the shells listed on the next page to match the name with the right picture. Write the name of the shell on the line under each picture.

1. Top Shell   2. Olive Shell

3. Angel Wing   4. Heart Cockle

5. Moon Shell   6. Cone Shell

(continued)

62

SCIENCE ACTIVITY

Olive Shell	Heart Cockle	Worm Shell
Top Shell	Angel Wing	Moon Shell
Tusk Shell	Slipper Shell	Volcano Limpet
Panther Cowrie	Spider Conch	Cone Shell

7. Spider Conch 8. Slipper Shell

9. Panther Cowrie 10. Volcano Limpet

11. Tusk Shell 12. Worm Shell

63

CRITICAL THINKING ACTIVITY

Are You a Good Detective?

How are your "seeing" powers? There are eight things wrong in the picture below. Can you detect all of them?

1. bicycle with no front wheel; 2. Yakko and Wakko on cannon; 3. Mime's shadow; 4. one way sign facing wrong way; 5. Sol's shoes—appliance store; 6. upside-down trashcan; 7. "e" missing from end of Pat's Grocery Store; 8. Ralph in winter clothes

64

McGraw-Hill Consumer Products

The skills taught in school are now available at home!
These award-winning software titles meet school guidelines and are based on
The McGraw-Hill Companies classroom software titles.

MATH GRADES 1 & 2

These math programs are a great way to teach and reinforce skills used in everyday situations. Fun, friendly characters need help with their math skills. Everyone's friend, Nubby the stubby pencil, will help kids master the math in the Numbers Quiz show. Foggy McHammer, a carpenter, needs some help building his playhouse so that all the boards will fit together! Julio Bambino's kitchen antics will surely burn his pastries if you don't help him set the clock timer correctly! We can't forget Turbo Tomato, a fruit with a passion for adventure, who needs help calculating his daredevil stunts.

Math Grades 1 & 2 use a tested, proven approach to reinforcing your child's math skills while keeping him or her intrigued with Nubby and his collection of crazy friends.

> TITLE
> Grade 1: Nubby's Quiz Show
> Grade 2: Foggy McHammer's Treehouse

MISSION MASTERS™ MATH AND LANGUAGE ARTS

The Mission Masters™—Pauline, Rakeem, Mia, and T.J.—need your help. The Mission Masters™ are a team of young agents working for the Intelliforce Agency, a high-level cooperative whose goal is to maintain order on our rather unruly planet. From within the agency's top secret Command Control Center, the agency's central computer, M5, has detected a threat...and guess what—you're the agent assigned to the mission!

MISSION MASTERS™ MATH GRADES 3, 4, & 5

This series of exciting activities encourages young mathematicians to challenge themselves and their math skills to overcome the perils of villains and other planetary threats. Skills reinforced include: analyzing and solving real-world problems, estimation, measurements, geometry, whole numbers, fractions, graphs, and patterns.

> TITLE
> Grade 3: Mission Masters™ Defeat Dirty D!
> Grade 4: Mission Masters™ Alien Encounter
> Grade 5: Mission Masters™ Meet Mudflat Moe

MISSION MASTERS™ LANGUAGE ARTS GRADES 3, 4, & 5

This series invites children to apply their language skills to defeat unscrupulous characters and to overcome other earthly dangers. Skills reinforced include: language mechanics and usage, punctuation, spelling, vocabulary, reading comprehension, and creative writing.

> TITLE
> Grade 3: Mission Masters™ Freezing Frenzy
> Grade 4: Mission Masters™ Network Nightmare
> Grade 5: Mission Masters™ Mummy Mysteries

BASIC SKILLS BUILDER K to 2 – THE MAGIC APPLEHOUSE

At the Magic Applehouse, children discover that Abigail Appleseed runs a deliciously successful business selling apple pies, tarts, and other apple treats. Enthusiasm grows as children join in the fun of helping Abigail run her business. Along the way they'll develop computer and entrepreneurial skills to last a lifetime. They will run their own business – all while they're having bushels of fun!

TITLE
Basic Skills Builder –The Magic Applehouse

TEST PREP – SCORING HIGH

This grade-based testing software will help prepare your child for standardized achievement tests given by his or her school. Scoring High specifically targets the skills required for success on the Stanford Achievement Test (SAT) for grades three through eight. Lessons and test questions follow the same format and cover the same content areas as questions appearing on the actual SAT tests. The practice tests are modeled after the SAT test-taking experience with similar directions, number of questions per section, and bubble-sheet answer choices.

Scoring High is a child's first-class ticket to a winning score on standardized achievement tests!

TITLE
Grades 3 to 5: Scoring High Test Prep
Grades 6 to 8: Scoring High Test Prep

SCIENCE

Mastering the principles of both physical and life science has never been so FUN for kids grades six and above as it is while they are exploring McGraw-Hill's edutainment software!

TITLE
Grades 6 & up: Life Science
Grades 8 & up: Physical Science

REFERENCE

The National Museum of Women in the Arts has teamed with McGraw-Hill Consumer Products to bring you this superb collection available for your enjoyment on CD-ROM.

This special collection is a visual diary of 200 women artists from the Renaissance to the present, spanning 500 years of creativity.

You will discover the art of women who excelled in all the great art movements of history. Artists who pushed the boundaries of abstract, genre, landscape, narrative, portrait, and still-life styles; as well as artists forced to push the societal limits placed on women through the ages.

TITLE
Women in the Arts

Most titles for Windows 3.1™, Windows '95™ & '98™, and Macintosh™.

Visit us on the Internet at:

www.MHkids.com

Or call 800-298-4119 for your local retailer.

McGraw-Hill Consumer Products

All our workbooks meet school curriculum guidelines and correspond to The McGraw-Hill Companies classroom textbooks.

SPECTRUM SERIES

DOLCH Sight Word Activities

The DOLCH Sight Word Activities Workbooks use the classic Dolch list of 220 basic vocabulary words that make up from 50% to 75% of all reading matter that children ordinarily encounter. Since these words are ordinarily recognized on sight, they are called *sight words*. Volume 1 includes 110 sight words. Volume 2 covers the remainder of the list. Over 160 pages.

TITLE	ISBN	PRICE
Grades K-1 Vol. 1	1-57768-429-X	$9.95
Grades K-1 Vol. 2	1-57768-439-7	$9.95

GEOGRAPHY

Full-color, three-part lessons strengthen geography knowledge and map reading skills. Focusing on five geographic themes including location, place, human/environmental interaction, movement, and regions. Over 150 pages. Glossary of geographical terms and answer key included.

TITLE	ISBN	PRICE
Gr 3, Communities	1-57768-153-3	$7.95
Gr 4, Regions	1-57768-154-1	$7.95
Gr 5, USA	1-57768-155-X	$7.95
Gr 6, World	1-57768-156-8	$7.95

MATH

Features easy-to-follow instructions that give students a clear path to success. This series has comprehensive coverage of the basic skills, helping children to master math fundamentals. Over 150 pages. Answer key included.

TITLE	ISBN	PRICE
Grade 1	1-57768-111-8	$6.95
Grade 2	1-57768-112-6	$6.95
Grade 3	1-57768-113-4	$6.95
Grade 4	1-57768-114-2	$6.95
Grade 5	1-57768-115-0	$6.95
Grade 6	1-57768-116-9	$6.95
Grade 7	1-57768-117-7	$6.95
Grade 8	1-57768-118-5	$6.95

PHONICS

Provides everything children need to build multiple skills in language. Focusing on phonics, structural analysis, and dictionary skills, this series also offers creative ideas for using phonics and word study skills in other language arts. Over 200 pages. Answer key included.

TITLE	ISBN	PRICE
Grade K	1-57768-120-7	$6.95
Grade 1	1-57768-121-5	$6.95
Grade 2	1-57768-122-3	$6.95
Grade 3	1-57768-123-1	$6.95
Grade 4	1-57768-124-X	$6.95
Grade 5	1-57768-125-8	$6.95
Grade 6	1-57768-126-6	$6.95

SPECTRUM SERIES – continued

READING

This full-color series creates an enjoyable reading environment, even for below-average readers. Each book contains captivating content, colorful characters, and compelling illustrations, so children are eager to find out what happens next. Over 150 pages. Answer key included.

TITLE	ISBN	PRICE
Grade K	1-57768-130-4	$6.95
Grade 1	1-57768-131-2	$6.95
Grade 2	1-57768-132-0	$6.95
Grade 3	1-57768-133-9	$6.95
Grade 4	1-57768-134-7	$6.95
Grade 5	1-57768-135-5	$6.95
Grade 6	1-57768-136-3	$6.95

SPELLING

This full-color series links spelling to reading and writing and increases skills in words and meanings, consonant and vowel spellings, and proofreading practice. Over 200 pages. Speller dictionary and answer key included.

TITLE	ISBN	PRICE
Grade 1	1-57768-161-4	$7.95
Grade 2	1-57768-162-2	$7.95
Grade 3	1-57768-163-0	$7.95
Grade 4	1-57768-164-9	$7.95
Grade 5	1-57768-165-7	$7.95
Grade 6	1-57768-166-5	$7.95

WRITING

Lessons focus on creative and expository writing using clearly stated objectives and pre-writing exercises. Eight essential reading skills are applied. Activities include main idea, sequence, comparison, detail, fact and opinion, cause and effect, and making a point. Over 130 pages. Answer key included.

TITLE	ISBN	PRICE
Grade 1	1-57768-141-X	$6.95
Grade 2	1-57768-142-8	$6.95
Grade 3	1-57768-143-6	$6.95
Grade 4	1-57768-144-4	$6.95
Grade 5	1-57768-145-2	$6.95
Grade 6	1-57768-146-0	$6.95
Grade 7	1-57768-147-9	$6.95
Grade 8	1-57768-148-7	$6.95

TEST PREP
From the Nation's #1 Testing Company

Prepares children to do their best on current editions of the five major standardized tests. Activities reinforce test-taking skills through examples, tips, practice, and timed exercises. Subjects include reading, math, and language. Over 150 pages. Answer key included.

TITLE	ISBN	PRICE
Grade 1	1-57768-101-0	$8.95
Grade 2	1-57768-102-9	$8.95
Grade 3	1-57768-103-7	$8.95
Grade 4	1-57768-104-5	$8.95
Grade 5	1-57768-105-3	$8.95
Grade 6	1-57768-106-1	$8.95
Grade 7	1-57768-107-X	$8.95
Grade 8	1-57768-108-8	$8.95

Visit us on the Internet at:
www.MHkids.com

RECEIVE THE McGRAW-HILL PARENT NEWSLETTER

FREE!

Thank you for expressing interest in the successful education of your child. With the purchase of this workbook, we know that you are committed to your child's development and future success. We at **McGraw-Hill Consumer Products** *would like to help you make a difference in the education of your child by offering a quarterly newsletter that provides current topics on education and activities that you and your child can work on together.*

To receive a free copy of our newsletter, please provide us with the following information:

Name _____

Address _____

City _____ State ____ Zip _____

e-mail (if applicable) _____

Store where book purchased _____

Grade Level of book purchased _____

Title of book purchased _____

Or visit us at:

Mail to:
Parent Newsletter
c/o McGraw-Hill Consumer Products
251 Jefferson Street, M.S. #12
Waldoboro, ME 04572

Or Call 800-298-4119

www.MHkids.com

This offer is limited to residents of the United States and Canada and is only in effect for as long as the newsletter is published.

The information that you provide will not be given, rented, or sold to any company.